Especially for

_____

From

_____

Date

_____

© 2011 by Barbour Publishing, Inc.

ISBN 978-1-61626-158-0

Compiled by Snapdragon Editorial Group℠, Tulsa, OK.

Several prayers are taken from *Prayers & Promises for Women* by Toni Sortor and *Prayers & Promises for Mothers* by Rachel Quillin and Nancy Farrier, published by Barbour Publishing, Inc.

Cover Credit: Cristina Cassinelli, Botanica, Getty Images

Published by Barbour Publishing, Inc., P.O. Box 719, Uhrichsville, Ohio 44683, www.barbourbooks.com

Our mission is to publish and distribute inspirational products offering exceptional value and biblical encouragement to the masses.

Member of the
Evangelical Christian
Publishers Association

Printed in China.

Prayers from the Heart

Inspiration for Every Day!

BARBOUR
PUBLISHING

The Peacekeeper

Lord, help me be the peacekeeper, never the one who stirs up more anger. Help me be an example to my whole family. Amen.

Patience

*Father, raising obedient, loving
children requires me to show
gentleness and patience, not threats
or harshness. I pray that You
will teach me how to soften each
correction with the same love
I receive from You. Amen.*

Strength to Forgive

Lord, give me the strength to forgive others so
You will forgive me my own trespasses. Amen.

Give Love

Lord, help me not to be quick to judge
or oppose love between others. Let me give
love time to do its work. I may never see
the result I want, but I am sure
it is in Your hands. Amen.

Have Mercy on Me

Have mercy on me, O God,
have mercy on me,
for in you my soul takes refuge.
I will take refuge in the
shadow of your wings.
Psalm 57:1 NIV

Thank You!

Father, thank You for all You have given me, for all You have taught me, and for all the good times still to come. Amen.

Purpose Revealed

When Your purpose is revealed to me, Father,
help me to accept my responsibility
and do Your will. Amen.

God's Power Can Overcome

Father, it often seems that might makes right and I stand no chance, but I know Your power can overcome whatever evil men might plan. When I am in despair, fill me with faith in Your justice. Amen.

Fill Me with Faith

I often feel that I lack faith, Lord,
that You must be speaking promises
for someone else—someone more
faithful and deserving of them.
Show me the error of this thinking.
Amen.

My Fortress

O my Strength, I watch for you;
you, O God, are my fortress,
my loving God.
God will go before me.
Psalm 59:9–10 NIV

Teach Me to Be Wise

Thank You, Lord, for what I do have,
which is happiness. Help me to be wise with
what money I have and use it in a way
that pleases You. Amen.

Keep Me from Temptation

Lord, I am human and often tempted.
Be with me when I am tempted and show
me the true joys of self-control. Amen.

Trust

Lord, I thank You for Your guidance
and protection day after day.
Although I never know what the
day will bring, You have a plan
and I trust in You. Amen.

Amen

Thank You for Motherhood

Thank You, Lord, that in Your perfect plan You've seen fit to give me beautiful children whom I probably don't deserve. Thank You for allowing me to be a mother. That is truly a gift from You. Amen.

My Rock

Turn your ear to me,
come quickly to my rescue;
be my rock of refuge,
a strong fortress to save me.

Psalm 31:2 NIV

Never Alone

Father, when troubles come,

I never have to face them alone.

Thank You for always being with me

as my refuge and strength.

When all else fails, I put my trust in You

and am never disappointed. Amen.

The Victor

Precious Father, on my own,
I am bound to fail. Now that I have
put my trust in You, I cannot fail,
for You are always the victor,
and this knowledge makes me
strong where once I was weak.
Amen.

A Virtuous Woman

Lord, I want to help bring others to You, to be judged a virtuous woman for Your sake, not for any glory that might come to me. Use me as You see fit, because any work You give me is an honor. Amen.

Make My Home a Blessing

Lord, I want my house to be Your house—
a house of prayer, a place of comfort and peace,
a refuge to those in need. Help me make our home
a blessing for all who pass through its door.

Amen.

Amen

Answer Me, O Lord

Do not let the floodwaters engulf me
or the depths swallow me up
or the pit close its mouth over me.
Answer me, O LORD,
out of the goodness of your love;
in your great mercy turn to me.

Psalm 69:15–16 NIV

My Time

Help me invest my time in more
worthy pursuits, Lord, ones that
will provide lasting satisfaction.
I'm not sure what You will ask of
me, but I am willing to try anything
You recommend and give any
resulting praise to You. Amen.

Much-Needed Courage

Father, when the time comes for me to release my children into Your care, give me the courage to do so graciously. Amen.

Grant Me Strength

Lord, I would prefer to live a life of peace,

but when I must fight for those I love,

I pray You will give me the strength to do so.

Amen.

Consolation and Comfort

Times of war are upon us, Father.
I ask for Your comfort for all the wives
and mothers who sit and wait, no matter on
what side their loved ones fight.
Thank You for Your consolation
and comfort. Amen.

Do Not Be Afraid

Do not be afraid! Don't be discouraged by this mighty army, for the battle is not yours, but God's.
2 Chronicles 20:15 NLT

A Better Future

*Father God, the joy has gone out
of my life. I need Your reassurance
that You will never give me a burden
without helping me bear it.
Be my strong hope of a better future.
Amen.*

Wisdom and Guidance

Father, I ask for Your wisdom and guidance.
Instruct me in the best ways to teach my children
about Your great love. I trust You will guide
me so I may serve You all the days of my life.
Amen.

Instruct My Children

Lord, help me teach all our children
about You, about Your great promises,
and about the peace that I pray will be
their inheritance. Amen.

In Time of Loss

I know that death comes to us all,
Lord, but sometimes I feel I cannot
give up a loved one. In time of loss,
send me Your comfort and peace,
I pray. Amen.

God's Ways

Your ways, O God, are holy.
What god is so great as our God?
You are the God who performs
miracles; you display your power
among the peoples.
Psalm 77:13–14 NIV

For All Things. . .

Thank You, Father, for giving us all the
things we need for life and godliness.
You are the Great Provider. Amen.

Sing Praises

I will praise you, O LORD,

with all my heart;

I will tell of all your wonders.

I will be glad and rejoice in you;

I will sing praise to your name,

O Most High.

Psalm 9:1–2 NIV

True Forgiveness

Father, show me the way to true forgiveness. I want to do Your will despite my weakness. Be my guide along this difficult path that leads to my own sorely needed forgiveness. Amen.

Blessing Others

*Lord Jesus, draw my family close to
You. Fill our home with Your presence
and our lives with Your love.
In turn, help each one of us to realize
the importance of blessing others.
Amen.*

Guidance for Children

Father, please give me the wisdom I need to properly advise my children. Help me teach them to seek guidance from Your Word and in communion with the Holy Spirit. Amen.

My Light

You are my lamp, O LORD;
the LORD turns my darkness into light.
With your help I can advance
against a troop; with my God
I can scale a wall.
2 Samuel 22:29–30 NIV

Just Right

Thank You, Lord, for being so faithful. Thank You for Your compassion—that is just the right amount to get me through the day. Amen.

True Contentment

Lord, show me how to be a godly woman, how to have true contentment that comes from service to You. Help me to reinforce in my home the need to be satisfied with doing Your will. Amen.

Today!

Lord, help me to rejoice in the time I have with my family today. I don't want to dwell on what might happen in the future; I want to relish this chance to nurture and cherish the blessings You've given me. Amen.

God Cares

Father, help me realize that my wants
are temporary and of little importance.
Let me lean against You, Lord, relaxed in
the knowledge that You will care for me.
Amen.

The Shepherd

*Save your people
and bless your inheritance;
be their shepherd
and carry them forever.*
Psalm 28:9 NIV

The Example

Thank You, Lord, for setting the example for me as a parent. There are times when I haven't listened. . .when I've done what I wanted to do, and You chastened me. It hurt, Lord, but I learned a valuable lesson. Amen.

Heavenly Witness

Lord, guide me so that all I am and do will point the way for others, that they also can enjoy the benefits of salvation and join their voices in praise of Your Father in heaven. Amen.

The Answers

Father, I know my understanding is weak.
But when I am in need of guidance,
the first place I turn to is Your Word.
Help me to search diligently, for I know
the answers I need are there. Amen.

With Love

Lord, I want to love the way You
do. I want to be strong, to lovingly
discipline my children so they
will grow to be pleasing to You.
No matter how difficult it is,
I will chastise with love. Amen.

Rejoice!

Let all who take refuge in you be glad;
let them ever sing for joy.
Spread your protection over them,
that those who love your name
may rejoice in you.
Psalm 5:11 NIV

Big and Small

Lord, thank You for every blessing, both big and small. Help me to be more aware of the ways in which You take care of me, so my gratitude can continue to grow. Amen.

Understanding

Lord, help me to be understanding with my children, to encourage rather than discourage. I want to take their hands and walk with them, as You've taken time to walk with me. Amen.

"Forever"

Forever, Lord—what encouragement
is in that word. We have all eternity
to spend with You in heaven.
Thank You for this indescribable
gift. Thank You for being the
Alpha and the Omega,
the first and the last. Amen.

God's Children

Lord, I'm grateful that I can show my children where to turn in times of trouble. They don't have to try to do it all themselves, because we are all Your children. Amen.

Your Hands. . .

Your hands made me and formed me;
give me understanding to learn your commmands.

Psalm 119:73 NIV

Let the Light Shine

Lord, if there's one thing I need,
it's trustworthy guidance. In darkness or
light, on fair days or foul, I trust that the
light of Your Word will bring me
safely home. Amen.

God's Will

Lord, help me to live according to
Your guidelines and show my kids
that Your plan is best as they strive
to live for You. Amen.

Advice

*Lord, show me my errors and teach
me the proper way to take advice.
Amen.*

For Good

Father, give me Your peace and an understanding
that all things work together for good when
I follow Your will. Amen.

Bless Us, O Lord

I have obeyed the LORD my God and have done everything you commanded me. Now look down from your holy dwelling place in heaven and bless your people.

Deuteronomy 26:14–15 NLT

Like You, Jesus

Lord, guide me daily to commit to being perfect. I know I can't expect my family to be perfect if I'm not willing to set the example. Help me as I strive to be like You. Amen.

Right Paths

*Father, Your Word contains the best
parenting instruction and advice
I could ever possess. Give me the
wisdom to weigh everything else
I read against what the Bible says.
Thank You for leading me in right
paths. Amen.*

Called to Be Godly

Lord, I'm called to live a godly life—
not by childishness but by Your grace and virtue.
Thank You for Your provision. Amen.

Be Glad

Teach us to number our days aright,

that we may gain a heart of wisdom.

Satisfy us in the morning with your

unfailing love, that we may sing for joy

and be glad all our days.

Psalm 90:12, 14 NIV

Attitude Adjustment

Lord, I need an attitude adjustment
that can only come from You.
Let me be a cheerful worker.
Resolve my conflicted feelings
and give me Your peace. Amen.

Keep Me Faithful

Lord, when times are hard and I become discouraged, be with me. Keep me a faithful teacher of the Way for the sake of my children and all those to come. Amen.

God's Representative

Lord, I know I am Your representative
here on earth and should give no one the
opportunity to reject You because of my actions.
When I am within seconds of being a
bad example, send me Your peace. Amen.

I Will Praise You

I will praise you, O LORD,

among the nations;

I will sing praises to your name.

2 Samuel 22:50 NIV

Sufficient Grace

Father, when I am a poor example
to someone I meet, grant me
forgiveness. Grant those I offend
the wisdom to understand that no
one is free of sin, but Your grace
is sufficient. Amen.

Faithful Companion

Be with all women living alone, Lord.
Be their faithful companion and guide
as they struggle to build a life based
on Your love and care. Amen.

A Godly Example

Lord, please give me the strength and the wisdom
to be the godly example that my children need
to see. I know that the life I live will have a
profound influence on the attitudes my children
develop concerning You. Amen.

Help Me to Live By Your Word

Lord, help me study Your Word and grow
in knowledge of You in order to attain
godliness. Then I can help my children
understand how to live godly lives. Amen.

Before Me

I have set the LORD always before me.
Because he is at my right hand,
I will not be shaken.
Psalm 16:8 NIV

A Constant Reminder

*As I read Your Word, it is a constant
reminder of Your love for me.
It also reminds me of how much You
love my kids and that You have their
best interest at heart. Amen.*

Heart Cleansing

Lord, let me know when I am wrong. That way I can come to You for cleansing and an opportunity to make things right. Thank You for the truth in Your Word, even though sometimes the truth hurts. Amen.

Teach Me to Relax

Heavenly Father, I find it hard to find
time to relax. Thank You for making me
to lie down even when I don't want to.
Thank You for leading me beside quiet
waters when I need the solace. Amen.

No Matter What

Lord, remove the fears that bind
me so that I can be happy in the
knowledge that You are there to
comfort me—no matter what else
is happening. Amen.

I Will Fear No Evil

*Even though I walk
through the valley of
the shadow of death,
I will fear no evil,
for you are with me;
your rod and your staff,
they comfort me.*
Psalm 23:4 NIV

Make Me an Instrument

Lord, I want to be instrumental in helping my family establish a close walk with You. Direct me daily to renew my commitment to follow in Your steps. Thank You for being the example I need. Amen.

Slowing Down

Father, I need rest—rest from my schedule,
rest from the demands of my family,
rest from "doing" to a place of simply
"being." Lead me to that place. Calm my
mind and my emotions so I can slow down
enough to find real rest. Amen.

Give and It Will Be Given unto You

Lord, You told me to give and that
if I do, it shall be given to me.
You don't say what "it" is, but Your
generosity is unmatched and Your
blessings are always wonderful.
Thank You! Amen.

The Best

Lord, I need Your gentle wisdom for every area of life. I'm so thankful that what You offer is the best. Amen.

Into Glory

You guide me with your counsel,
and afterward you will take me into glory.
Psalm 73:24 NIV

To Be Gentle

Father, You gave me my children to cherish,
and that includes being gentle with them.
I do treasure them, Lord, so help me to
impart Your gentleness to them. Amen.

Joy and Strength

Thank You, God, for Your Word.
It instructs me how to live.
It brings joy to my days and gives
me strength when I am weak.
Amen.

How to Trust

Lord, I'm ashamed to admit that sometimes I have a hard time taking You at Your Word. Please show me how to trust You more, even when my mind can't grasp it and my heart can't accept it. Amen.

Listen Up

Father, I get discouraged when I don't know
which way to go. Remind me that You are right
behind me, telling me which way to turn.
Help me to be quiet and listen for Your guidance.

Amen.

Not Shaken

Find rest, O my soul, in God alone;
my hope comes from him.
He alone is my rock and my salvation;
he is my fortress, I will not be shaken.
Psalm 62:5-6 NIV

The Good Shepherd

Father, Your guidance is
trustworthy. You are our Good
Shepherd. You lead us to places
of rest when we need them.
My children and I need that rest.
Thank You for Your leading. Amen.

Be Joyful

There's no mistaking, Lord.
You've made it clear that I'm to
be joyful in each and every task.
The next time I'm tempted to
complain about the mounds of work,
remind me to turn the murmuring
into praise. Amen.

Reflecting Glory

Gracious Father, I thank You for the work
I have. May I do it in a way that is pleasing
to You and that reflects Your glory. Amen.

Priorities

Father, praising You and rejoicing in
You must be high on my priority list.
Proclaiming Your love to others must never
be lacking in my life. Thank You that
I am able to rejoice in You! Amen.

A Close Walk

Father God, joy fills my life when
my son asks to have a book read
and then chooses one about You.
I pray that this is the beginning of
a close walk that he will eventually
have with You. Amen.

Teach Me Your Way

Teach me your way, O Lord,
and I will walk in your truth;
give me an undivided heart,
that I may fear your name.
Psalm 86:11 NIV

Always Ready

Father, I don't know how You will use my life,
but I have faith in Your promises and am always
ready to do Your will. Amen.

A Friend

I love my children, Lord. I thank You for
them, but sometimes I need another person
to talk to who understands what I'm going
through. Help me find a friend—someone
who needs the kind of companionship I do.
Amen.

Forgive Me, Lord

Forgive me, Lord, for those times
when I've doubted Your love.
Let me close my eyes, hold out
my hand, and know that You are
there. Thank You for being with me,
Father. Amen.

An Ambassador

*I am Your ambassador, Lord,
and every day I try to show Your
love to those who do not know You.
I pray that when the time comes,
You will find me worthy. Amen.*

Hear My Voice

Hear my voice in accordance with your love;
preserve my life, O LORD, according to your laws.
Psalm 119:149 NIV

Teach Me to Discipline

Father, I want my children to know
what I expect of them and then obey.
Give me guidance to establish the
right reward and discipline system.
I need strength in that area, Lord. Amen.

Patience by Example

Still my complaining heart, Lord. Fill me with rejoicing. I want to teach my children patience by my own example. Give me strength for the task. Amen.

Blessed Abundantly

Father, I know You blessed me abundantly in the family You have given me. Help me not to flaunt them or to take the credit that belongs to You. Amen.

Steadfast and Dedicated

Father, my daily problems come and go;
yet if I remain steadfast and dedicated,
doing the work You have given me to do,
I am confident that my reward awaits me.
Thank You, Lord. Amen.

Remember the Miracles

*I will remember the deeds of the LORD;
yes, I will remember your miracles of long
ago. I will meditate on all your works
and consider all your mighty deeds.*

Psalm 77:11–12 NIV

"Inner Power"

Lord, I can see Your inner power at work in my children as they grow in You. Your Spirit inside us is a life-changing power that will always be available to us wherever we are. Thank You for this wonderful gift. Amen.

Cleansed by the Blood

*I've made mistakes, Lord.
But someday You will present me
faultless, cleansed by Your blood.
The evidence of Your power to lift me
up and make me whole fills me with
exceeding joy. I praise You forever and
forever. Amen.*

Always Sufficient

I sometimes want to rely on my power rather than Yours, Lord. I pray that my children will witness that Your grace is always sufficient. When we are weak, then we will be strong in You. Amen.

Song of Joy

Put a new song in my mouth, Lord.
Let others see me being patient and waiting
on You, no matter what difficulty I'm
facing. Help them learn the same song of joy
that You are giving me. Amen.

The Lord Is with You!

Stand still and watch the Lord's victory. He is with you, O people of Judah and Jerusalem. Do not be afraid or discouraged. Go out against them tomorrow, for the Lord is with you!
2 Chronicles 20:17 NLT

Visible Patience and Kindness

Lord, I ask for Your help in raising my children. May Your patience and kindness be made visible through my actions. Amen.

Faithfulness

Father, give me faithfulness in all things large
and small, so that I may be an example to my
children and a blessing to my husband—
and to all those near me. Amen.

Completion of God's Plan

Lord, help me realize that my understanding
is not necessary for the completion of
Your plan. You understand everything;
all I need to do is have faith. Amen.

Fairness

Lord, help me not to judge, but to let
You decide the fairness of matters.
Give me patience—to rest in You
and to wait for Your return.
I need Your help to teach my
children to rest in You, too. Amen.

Our Protector

You hear, O LORD,
the desire of the afflicted;
you encourage them,
and you listen to their cry,
defending the fatherless
and the oppressed,
in order that man,
who is of the earth,
may terrify no more.

Psalm 10:17–19 NIV

Answered Prayer

Lord, when I see how You have interceded on my behalf, I want to fall on my face before You. My prayers have been answered in miraculous ways. In times when all I could see was darkness, you provided light and power and hope. Amen.

Count It All Joy

Lord, You are made strong in my weaknesses.
I need Your help to remember that and teach
my children that we should count it all joy
when we are faced with trials and suffering.
Amen.

Without Fear

Lord, the next time I am faced
with danger for Your sake,
let me remember that You are
faithful to reward Your people,
no matter how much I may fear.
Amen.

Never Forsaken

There are times, Lord, when I feel as if You've forgotten me. How could I let those feelings of being forsaken overwhelm me? Help me to remember that the Creator of the entire universe holds me in His hands! Amen.

Worthy

I call to the LORD, who is worthy of praise,
and I am saved from my enemies.
Psalm 18:3 NIV

Eternal Promise

Thank You for Your promise to preserve me if I love You, Father. I know that this is an eternal promise. What more incentive do I need to pursue a right walk with You? Keep me on the right path, Lord. Amen.

True Love

Thank You, Jesus, for Your sacrificial love for me. Thank You for the example of true love that You have provided. Amen.

Assurance

*Lord, help me to put aside my
needs, to draw my child close,
and to assure him of my love and,
more importantly, of Your love. Amen.*

A Servant's Heart

Father, I need a reminder that what I should be is a servant. I get so wrapped up in the need to maintain order that I forget my job—to meet the needs of my family. Please give me a servant's heart. Amen.

A Willing Spirit

Restore to me the joy of your salvation
and grant me a willing spirit, to sustain me.
Psalm 51:12 NIV

Small Beauty

Father, please don't let me fall
into the trap of false pride.
Whatever small beauty I bring into
this world is only a tiny reflection
of Your beauty, Your creation,
Your perfection. Amen.

A Team

Father, teach my husband and me to work as a team in raising our children, sharing the good times and the bad, so that neither of us should be overburdened. Amen.

Comforting Opportunities

Dear Jesus, in this world it is certain that there will be many opportunities to offer comfort to my little ones. Help me to always be there for them to comfort them as You comfort me. Amen.

Loving Arms

Father, I can't begin to count the number of times You've wrapped Your loving arms around me and calmed me in the midst of fears. You've drawn me near in times of sorrow and given me assurance when I've faced great disappointment. Amen.

Safe

*For in the day of trouble
he will keep me safe in his dwelling;
he will hide me in the shelter
of his tabernacle and set me
high upon a rock.*
Psalm 27:5 NIV

Serving

Heavenly Father, I want my children to serve You, but I know they can only do that if they have true faith in You. Help me live so that they will want this kind of faith. Amen.

Teachable Moments

Lord, as a mother, I need to take advantage of the teachable moments You give me to teach my children the truths about Your Word. I pray that with Your help, I'll never let an opportunity pass by.

Amen.

All I Need

Father, on days when I go off on my own, draw me close to You until I calm down and begin to think clearly. Everything is under control. All I need has been provided. Thank You. Amen.

My Hope

Lord, You are my hope in an often hopeless world. You are my hope of heaven, my hope of peace, my hope of change, purpose, and unconditional love. Fill the reservoir of my heart to overflowing with the joy that real hope brings. Amen.

All Day Long

Show me your ways, O LORD,
teach me your paths;
guide me in your truth and teach me,
for you are God my Savior,
and my hope is in you all day long.
Psalm 25:4–5 NIV

The Fruits of My Labor

When I grow old, Lord, I pray that I will see the fruits of my labor and rejoice, knowing that all my efforts were well worth the time and energy I put into them. Amen.

Comfort Me

When grief comes to me, Father, I know
You will understand if I turn my face
away from everyone for a time. I know You
understand my suffering and long to comfort
me. Amen.

Parenting God's Way

Lord, You've given me plenty of
instruction on parenting, and it's
because You know what's best.
Thank You for seeing the need to
include parenting in Your Word.
Amen.

Small Ways

Father, there are certain children whom I do not want to let into my house because of bad behavior. Show me how I can help guide them in some small way without taking over their parents' duties. Amen.

According to Your Love

Preserve my life according to your love,
and I will obey the statutes of your mouth.
Psalm 119:88 NIV

Through the Eyes of a Child

I know my children have a lot to teach me,
Lord. Help me be receptive to Your lessons,
especially when You send them
through a child. Amen.

Pleasures

Lord, thank You for Your gift of physical pleasures, but teach us to use them wisely, according to Your wishes for us. Keep us faithful to our spouses and to Your laws of self-control. Amen.

Victory

Lord, show me the path to victory every day, because sometimes I find it hard to follow. You know every turn in the road, and I will follow You in security all the days of my life. Amen.

A Woman of Value

Thank You for the work You have given me, Father, with its opportunities to be of service to others and to You. You have made me a woman of value, and my contribution is great. Amen.

I Lift Up My Soul

Let the morning bring me word of your
unfailing love, for I have put my trust in
you. Show me the way I should go,
for to you I lift up my soul.

Psalm 143:8 NIV

A Child Light

Lord Jesus, You have paid for my
salvation through Your death on the
cross. You made me a child of light
that I might guide others to You.
You have made me worthy,
and I thank You. Amen.

Obedience

Lord, I want to obey You in everything and also lead my children to obey You. Through our obedience to You, help us to reach many people for Your kingdom. Amen.

Learning to Obey

Father, I need to show my children how important obedience is by being obedient myself—to You and to others in authority over me. Thank You for assisting me in this effort. Amen.

Unconditional Love

I am proud of my children, Lord,
but I don't want this pride to be wicked or
foolish; rather, let it be the motherly type
that is based on unconditional love. Amen.

Bring Joy

Bring joy to your servant,
for to you, O Lord,
I lift up my soul.
Psalm 86:4 NIV

Continual Praise

Today in anger, I said something I shouldn't have. Forgive me, Lord. Instead of speaking in anger and frustration, I want to fill my mouth with words of continual praise to You. Amen.

A Living Sacrifice

Lord, make me a living sacrifice for You,
that I might lead my children and others to You.
Let my praises be a godly example in my home.
I praise You with all that is within me. Amen.

The Gift

Lord, one of the greatest gifts You've given me is the Holy Spirit to intercede for me during prayer. Thank You, Holy Spirit, for intervening and making my requests better than I ever could. Amen.

A Beautiful Family

Thank You for granting my request and blessing me with a beautiful family. I give my children back to You. I ask that You would use each one for Your glory. Amen.

Serving You, Lord

Lord, help my children to dedicate themselves to serving You in whatever capacity You would call them. Amen.

With All My Heart

Teach me, O LORD, to follow your decrees;
then I will keep them to the end.
Give me understanding, and I will keep your
law and obey it with all my heart.
Psalm 119:33–34 NIV

Redefining Greatness

Lord, help me to redefine "greatness" for my
children and show them worthy examples of
those who have received You.
They need to know that there is a better,
more glorious way to live. Amen.

A Merry Heart

Father, help me to get over
self-doubt. Remind me that
Your blessings are forever and
I have nothing to fear. Give me
a merry heart. Amen.

Provision

*Lord, thank You for Your attention
to those who struggle,
for Your provision, and for the
promise that their dreams will
eventually come true. I wish them
the contentment I am now enjoying.
Amen.*

The Best Approach

Father, help me see when my children need gentle,
loving correction, and show me the best approach.
Let me be as kind and patient with my children
as You are with me. Amen.

Good Things

When we were overwhelmed by sins,
you forgave our transgressions.
Blessed are those you choose
and bring near to live in your courts!
We are filled with the good things of
your house, of your holy temple.
Psalm 65:3-4 NIV

To Be Humble

Father, You've given me the wonderful task of being a mother. Help me to do the job humbly and to rely on You. That is what would please You most, and that reward is the best motivator I could ask for. Amen.

Surrounded by Love

*Lord, Your promise of protection gives
me a secure feeling. I'm surrounded
by Your love and protection.
Because You love me and care for me,
I can do the same for my children.
Thank You for the peace this brings.
Amen.*

The Mighty One

Father, as long as I trust in Your presence,
I have nothing to worry about.
Nothing can separate me from You, because
You are the strong protector, the mighty One
who watches over me always. I praise You,
Lord, for Your protection. Amen.

A Perfect Heart

Make my heart perfect, Lord.
Take my hand, and give me strength.
Be strong for me when I don't measure up.
My way to attain a perfect heart is through
You, Lord, so don't take Your eyes off me.
Amen.

The Upright in Heart

Do good, O LORD,
to those who are good,
to those who are upright in heart.
Psalm 125:4 NIV

To Be Pure

Lord, on days when I'm having spiritual struggles, my thoughts become full of discouragement and frustration. I don't like to be so controlled by my emotions. Please give me the strength to be pure in every situation. Amen.

Reflections

Lord, help me realize that everything my husband says about me does not always reflect his true feelings. When his words hurt me, show me how to explain this to him. I am "a good thing" — I deserve to be treated with respect. Amen.

Control My Tongue, Lord

Lord, in the heat of anger, control my tongue, because what I say then can be as damaging to my soul as it is to my victim's reputation. Amen.

Made Worthy

Lord, You stand before the throne of Your Father and claim me as Your own, exempt from sin and judgment. Because of Your sacrifice, I am made worthy. Thank You. Amen.

Blameless

*Keep your servant also from willful
sins; may they not rule over me.
Then will I be blameless,
innocent of great transgression.*
Psalm 19:13 NIV

For Answered Prayers

Father, please protect my children from spiritual and physical harm, and give them sound minds and bodies. I thank You in advance for answered prayers. Amen.

What a Blessing!

Thank You, Lord, for putting other godly moms in my life. They face many temptations that I face, but they've committed themselves to purity, so together we can encourage one another. What a blessing! Amen.

Focus

Father, I know that I tend to get
focused on the negatives,
and sometimes my thoughts are
crowded with impatience, envy,
anger, or resentment.
Please help me focus on You.
Fill me with pure thoughts. Amen.

Patient Endurance

Thank You, Lord. You have given me a wonderful example of patient endurance. When I am losing patience with my children, I recall how long You waited for me to repent and turn to You. Amen.

Your Name, O Lord

For the sake of your name, O LORD,
forgive my iniquity, though it is great.
Psalm 25:11 NIV

Help Me to Wait

Father, when my children do wrong,
I want them to admit it and ask for
forgiveness. From Your example with me,
I know there are times I need to wait for
my children's repentance. Help me wait,
Lord. Amen.

Heal Me, Lord

Thank You for the times I am humbled, Lord. You are always here—to listen, to forgive, and to heal. Lord, help me to be repentant, to be willing to be brought low. Heal me, Lord. Amen.

The Right Example

*Lord, when I am old, I want my
children to respect and love me.
By my actions toward others,
I am always teaching—either respect
or disrespect. I want to set the right
example for my children as I honor
older people. Amen.*

Humble Me

Humble me, Lord. Fill me with the desire to hearken to my parents. I can learn so much from them and benefit from their life experiences. I believe this is Your will. Thank You for Your patience and guidance. Amen.

On Level Ground

Teach me to do your will,
for you are my God;
may your good Spirit
lead me on level ground.
Psalm 143:10 NIV

Great Expectations

Lord, You've given me a life that
abounds with rich blessings,
and You've guaranteed that
because of this You also have great
expectations of me. Help me to
be faithful to these expectations.
Amen.

The Humble Spirit

Heavenly Father, we live in a world that lifts up proud people. Make us all aware of how much You value sacrifice. Help us to have the humble spirit we need when we come before You. Amen.

For Your Mercy

Thank You, Jesus, for calling sinners to repentance. If You had come only for the righteous, I would not have been called, for I am a sinner. I thank You for Your mercy. Amen.

The Blessing of Family

Father, thank You for granting my request
and blessing me with a beautiful family.
My prayer now is that each of my children
would accept You as their personal Savior.
Then I ask that You would use each one
for Your glory. Amen.

Deliver Us

*Help us, O God our Savior,
for the glory of your name;
deliver us and forgive our sins
for your name's sake.*
Psalm 79:9 NIV

In Song

*Father, make me mindful of Your
great gifts, that my song may praise
Your work in my life. Amen.*

Character and Courage

Lord, sometimes I have to take a stand,
no matter what happens. When these times come,
I pray you will give me character and courage.
Amen.

Everywhere

Lord, there is so much I do not understand about You. Still, I can see the effects of Your actions, the evidence that You are still active in my daily life. I do not need to physically see You to believe.
Your evidence is everywhere. Amen.

Whole

Father, the life I am living right now
is not the result of my faith in You
but of Your faith in me.
Thank You for Your sacrifice that
saves me and makes me whole.
Amen.

A Pure Heart

Hide your face from my sins
and blot out all my iniquity.
Create in me a pure heart, O God,
and renew a steadfast spirit within me.
Psalm 51:9–10 NIV

Example of Compassion

Lord, help me to show compassion for my children
and also for strangers. You were the best example.
You loved everyone, Lord. Help me do the same,
and in doing so set an example for my children.

Amen.

Shout Praises

Lord, I don't know if I'll ever understand
why You sacrificed Yourself for me.
But, from the depths of my being, I want to
shout praises to You and also tell the whole
world what You did for all of us. Amen.

A Life of Sacrifice

I want my life to be a sacrifice for You, Lord. Help me live a life of praise for You before my children. Guide me in showing my children how to make the sacrifice of praise to You. Amen.

Wonderful Gifts

Heavenly Father, help me show my children the way to You while they are so eager to learn. I want to teach them about Your grace and mercy— the wonderful gifts You've made available to everyone. Amen.

Heaven and Earth

O LORD, God of Israel, enthroned between the
cherubim, you alone are God over all the kingdoms
of the earth. You have made heaven and earth.
2 Kings 19:15 NIV

A Joyful Noise

Lord, You are my strength and my song.
Help me teach my children to sing,
no matter what is going on around us.
I want us to make a joyful noise to You,
Jesus, the author and finisher of our faith.
Amen.

Spiritual Growth

Lord, I really want to grow spiritually. I need to—for my own daily walk with You and, most importantly, because You've commanded me to. Thank You for giving me the strength to fulfill your commands and to grow spiritually. Amen.

Self-Control

Father, Your Holy Spirit is telling me that self-control is not one of my strengths and I need to work on it. I need temperance. Help me turn things over to You and allow You to develop self-control in my life. Amen.

Quiet My Spirit

Lord, there's so much chaos. Quiet my spirit.
Let me close my eyes for a moment and experience
Your touch. My strength comes from You,
not from any other source. Calm me. Keep me
anchored in You and Your Spirit. Amen.

Know My Heart

Search me, O God, and know my heart;

test me and know my anxious thoughts.

See if there is any offensive way in me,

and lead me in the way everlasting.

Psalm 139:23–24 NIV

Perfect Parenting

Lord, when I first considered
starting a family, I thought I would
be a perfect parent. It was easier
dreamed than done. I know I need
Your assistance if I'm going to be
a good mother. I'm so grateful for
Your guidance. Amen.

God's Strength

*Because of Your strength, Lord,
I can smile. When I need peace,
You strengthen me on the inside.
This is where I need You the most.
Let me reflect Your strength so that
my children will be drawn to You also.
Amen.*

An Army

You are like an army, Lord, surrounding me with
Your strength and power. I don't have to depend
on my limited might and abilities. Teach me to
draw on Your strength. Amen.

Blessed Promise

Father, physically, I'm wearing out.
But in the core of my being, in my heart,
I still feel strengthened by You. What a
blessed promise that this inner strength will
be my portion forever. Amen.

Awesome God

You are awesome, O God,
in your sanctuary;
the God of Israel gives power
and strength to his people.
Praise be to God!
Psalm 68:35 NIV

Strong in Faith

*Lord, keep me strong in my faith,
no matter what. When I am following
You, I can be blessed, no matter what
others say about me.
Thank You, Jesus, for mapping the
way for me and for my children.
Amen.*

Exceeding Joy

Father, help me to remember that my children's suffering is every bit as real to them as mine is to me. I need to be compassionate, to show them that they will experience exceeding joy because of these trials. Amen.

That Wonderful Day

Lord, I know there will come a day when we will be in heaven with You. I look forward to that time, and I thank You for the opportunity to share that time and place with You. Amen.

Creative Delight

Father, I want to make You exciting
and interesting to my children.
Give me creative ideas as we
take walks, clean the house, do
schoolwork, or engage in other
routine activities. I pray it will be a
delight for all of us. Amen.

We Give Thanks

We give thanks to you,
Lord God Almighty,
the One who is and who was,
because you have taken your great
power and have begun to reign.
Revelation 11:17 NIV

Fill My Heart

Give me wisdom, Lord. I want to teach my children Your Word so that we can teach and admonish one another with scripture. Fill my heart with Your love, so that my teaching will reflect You. Amen.

Eyes on Jesus

In the midst of suffering, I want to keep my eyes on You, Jesus. The suffering You endured for my sake makes my trials look like nothing. Help me look forward to the promise and to forget the temporary troubles I have now. Amen.

Understanding and Trust

Father, help me understand
faithfulness and to trust in Your
love above all else, claiming none
of Your glory as a personal reward.
Amen.

What a Wonderful Name!

*Jesus. What a wonderful name!
It is the only name we need to call
upon for salvation. I praise You for
being the Way, the Truth, and the Life,
Lord. Amen.*

The Good Times

Lord, I ask for Your help when it comes to getting along with my family members. Teach me to focus on the good times we had together, not the bad, and to concentrate on their good points for the sake of family peace. Amen.

Day 212

Unfailing Love

I trust in your unfailing love;
my heart rejoices in your salvation.
Psalm 13:5 NIV

With Joy

I am not worthy of Your gifts of
mercy and forgiveness, Father,
but I accept them with joy. Amen.

Eternal Blessings

Father, Your correction lasts only a moment; but its blessings are eternal. When I realize You are so concerned for me and want to help me, I am filled with gratitude and willing to be led in the right direction. Amen.

Sharing the Gift

Heavenly Father, my greatest responsibility as
Your child is to share the gift of salvation with
others. My family, my neighbors, my children—
so many people need to hear Your Word.
Make me attentive to each opportunity You
present to me. Amen.

Secure in Love

Father, when my time on earth comes to an end, I pray I will be able to bear death as well as I bore life, secure in Your love and looking to the salvation that You have promised is mine. Amen.

One True God

O LORD, God of Israel, there is no God like you in heaven above or on earth below—you who keep your covenant of love with your servants who continue wholeheartedly in your way.
1 Kings 8:23 NIV

Daily Blessings

*You bless my life in many ways
every day, Father. May I receive Your
blessings with a song of thanksgiving
on my lips. Amen.*

Confidence

Father, cleanse me from my ungrounded fears.
Fill me with confidence that I can share with
my children. You are the strong protector.
I am thankful that, because of Jesus,
we will be lifted up as the stones in a crown.
Amen.

Standing Firm

Lord, show my children what convictions to
establish and give them the strength to stand
firm in those convictions. Amen.

A Light to Others

Lord, may those I work with always
see You in my life and be brought
closer to You though me. Amen.

Unfailing Love

*May your unfailing love
rest upon us, O LORD,
even as we put our hope in you.*
Psalm 33:22 NIV

The Promise

Thank You for Your promise to guide me in all things great and small. Your eye is always on me, keeping me from error and ensuring that I can always find a way home to You. Amen.

His Mighty Arms

When my time comes to grieve, Lord,
be with me. Hold me up with Your mighty
arms until I can stand on my own once more.
Hasten the passing of my season of grief.
Amen.

You Know the Way, Lord

Lord, I do not know how to deliver
myself from temptation,
but You know the way. You have
been there. When I stumble, I know
Your arms will catch me; if I fall,
You bring me to my feet and guide
me onward. Amen.

Full Hearts

Father, fill our hearts full of You and Your Word; then we can sing with grace and joy. My family and I can proclaim Your goodness to all those we meet. What a blessing! Amen.

Great Peace

Great peace have they who love your law,
and nothing can make them stumble.
Psalm 119:165 NIV

Peace, Forgiveness, and Love

Lord, forgive me when I treat my family
members poorly. Show me their good points,
for I have overlooked or forgotten many of
them. For the sake of our parents,
our children, and ourselves, help me bring
peace, forgiveness, and love to our family.
Amen.

Simple Service

Father, there comes a time in every woman's life when her parents begin to need help. Give me the wisdom to understand the problems they are having and the often simple ways I can be of service to them. Amen.

Constantly Blessed

Lord, I know bad things will come my way in life, but I am secure in Your love that never fails. I am constantly blessed by Your care and concern. I am so important to You that even the hairs of my head are all numbered. Amen.

Beyond Beauty

Lord, teach me to look beyond appearance when
I choose my friends or my husband. Help me see
beyond beauty—or lack of it. Amen.

He Is Worthy

You are worthy, our Lord and God,
to receive glory and honor and power,
for you created all things,
and by your will they were created
and have their being.

Revelation 4:11 NIV

Money Matters

Father, when it comes to money matters, I cannot approach perfection, but I know with Your help I can learn to handle our family finances faithfully. Amen.

Father, Direct Me

Father, direct me in how to be involved in the lives of my children. Help me build on Your teachings by setting the right example, praying for them, being there for them, and caring for them. Amen.

The Call of Motherhood

Lord, I believe the call to motherhood comes from You. Help me approach my calling with a meek and humble spirit. Only when my outlook becomes Christlike will I truly be considered worthy of this calling. Amen.

Special Love

Father, sometimes I forget to show my
children how important they are.
Let Your love fill my heart so that it pours
over and floods the children You've so
graciously given me. Help me show them
how special they are to me. Amen.

Marvelous Things

O Lord, you are my God;
I will exalt you and praise your name,
for in perfect faithfulness
you have done marvelous things,
things planned long ago.
Isaiah 25:1 NIV

Hear My Cries

Lord, I want to learn to be patient and trust in You. I know that You will hear my cries and I will be blessed. Thank You for this blessing. Amen.

Honor

Father, sometimes I have to go against the wishes
of others to do Your will, and it's not always
pleasant, but Your wishes come before all others,
and I will do my best to honor Your name
all my days. Amen.

Never on My Own

Lord, I know that You are the one at work
in me; Your Spirit is a part of me,
and You guide my thoughts and actions.
Thank You for that. I don't know what I
would do if I had to live life on my own.
Amen.

Renew Me

As I learn to rest in You, Lord,
renew me. Give me the ability I
need to be patient, no matter what
trouble is around me. Let my joyful
hope and faithful prayers build up
my patience. Amen.

Mold Me

Lord, help me to draw my children close when that's needed and to become involved in their play when that would be better. Mold me into the mother they need. Amen.

Strength for Difficult Times

Lord, in time, I may have to begin to play a
more active role in the lives of my aging parents.
This can be a difficult time for all of us.
I ask for Your help and guidance when
this time comes. Amen.

Day 244

Cast Your Cares

*Cast your cares on the LORD
and he will sustain you;
he will never let the righteous fall.*

Psalm 55:22 NIV

Fill Me with Comfort

Father, my heart is breaking over
the death of someone I love.
Fill me with Your comfort and the
joy that comes from knowing that
when death does come, You will
be there to guide us home to You.
Amen.

Direct Me Daily

Lord, direct me daily to accept and apply the strength that You've offered, so that I will truly have the gentle spirit that You intended me to have. Thank You, Jesus, that I don't have to do this on my own. Amen.

Nothing Is Impossible

Father, quite often I pray for what is impossible.
But for You, nothing is impossible. Amen.

Day 248

With God. . .

Jesus looked at them intently and said,
"Humanly speaking, it is impossible.
But not with God. Everything is
possible with God."
Mark 10:27 NLT

Something Special

Heavenly Father, I pray that my children will love Your Word and understand how special they are to You and that You have something for each of them to meditate on each day. Amen.

Incline My Heart

*Lord, help me to be as generous to
my family as I am to strangers.
Give me Your guidance. Reveal the
needs of my brother and sister—
whether they are physical, emotional,
or spiritual—and incline my heart
to them. Amen.*

Supportive

Father, help me remember that my priorities are
not necessarily the priorities of those I love,
so please give me the sense to step back and allow
everyone a little leeway to lead their own lives.
Help me be supportive, not bossy. Amen.

My Hope

Lord, I know not all prayers are answered,
but many are, so I continue to petition You,
for You are my hope. Amen.

Hear Me, God

Listen to my prayer, O God,
do not ignore my plea;
hear me and answer me.
Psalm 55:1–2 NIV

Our Nation's Leaders

Lord, we are a hurt nation—an angry nation struggling to maintain its values while still dealing firmly with those who hate us. Guide our nation's leaders during these difficult times. We trust in You and long for peace. Amen.

Never Hesitate

Lord, may I never hesitate to forgive anyone when
You have already forgiven me. Amen.

God's Timetable

Father, help me to have patience,
knowing my season is coming according to
Your timetable and trusting that with Your
help, every fruit I produce will be good.
Amen.

Free Offer of Compassion

Lord, sometimes compassion is all a
person needs to gain strength.
I pray I will always offer it freely.
Amen.

Remembering God's Ways

*You come to the help of those
who gladly do right,
who remember your ways.*
Isaiah 64:5 NIV

Wisely. . .

Lord, as my parents age and need more help from
me, remind me that other help is available.
You have provided these helpers for us;
let us use them wisely. Amen.

Encouragers

Lord, help me to teach my children that to
grow as encouragers they can start with
small things as they comfort others and build
from there. Amen.

Through You, Lord

Through You, Lord, I can live a life
that will give others no right to
accuse me of any wrongdoing.
I pray that You'll allow my life to
be an example that will encourage
my family, friends, and others to
come to You. Amen.

The Patience to Wait

Lord, help me overcome the urge to pat myself on the back in the sight of others and wait to hear You say, "Well done." Amen.

His Love Endures Forever

The LORD will fulfill his purpose for me;
your love, O LORD, endures forever—
do not abandon the works of your hands.

Psalm 138:8 NIV

Pleasing God

Father, be with us today and stay near as we strive to raise our family in a way that will please You and allow us to accomplish whatever You have planned. Amen.

Overcoming Fears

Lord, being a mother is causing
me to worry and be fearful.
Thank You for helping me overcome
my "mother" fears. Life is too
wonderful not to enjoy. Amen.

A Blessing

Lord, help me work to be a blessing to those around me in my daily life. Amen.

Vows

Vows to You must be kept, Father. You not only remember Your promises to us, You never forget our promises to You. Help me treat my vows to You seriously, Lord. If sacrifices are required of me, let me bear them in faith. Amen.

An Everlasting Kingdom

Your kingdom is an everlasting kingdom,
and your dominion endures through all
generations. The LORD is faithful to all his
promises and loving toward all he has made.

Psalm 145:13 NIV

Atmosphere of Love

Lord, help me give my husband the aid and support he needs. His life is hard, and he deserves to live in an atmosphere of love and security. Amen.

Restoring Harmony

Lord, give me the resolve to make things better, to ignore my pride, and to do whatever is needed to restore the harmony in my family. Amen.

Confidence in His Promises

Lord, give me confidence in Your promises so I
may never worry about the welfare of my children,
whom You love even more than I do and have
promised to care for. Amen.

Appreciation

Father, thank You for helping us to raise
children who appreciate what they have and
work hard to build their own lives,
with or without financial riches. Amen.

Acts of Charity

Lord, help me to be charitable in all that I do. My acts of charity reflect on You, and I want to bring honor to You at all times. Amen.

In My Heart

I have hidden your word in my heart
that I might not sin against you.
Psalm 119:11 NIV

Always Right

Father, I admit that once in a while I have
a temper tantrum, disputing Your guidance and
wanting my own way, but You have never been
wrong. Thank You for Your love and patience,
for I will always need Your guidance.
Amen.

Today and Tomorrow

Lord, keep me on the right path when my own plans are flawed, because only You know where You need me to be today and tomorrow.

Amen.

Home

Lord, I often make mistakes on the
path of life, losing sight of the trail
and calling out for You.
Thank You for finding me, for
putting my feet back on the path
and leading me home. Amen.

Free Me

*Since you are my rock
and my fortress,
for the sake of your name
lead and guide me.
Free me from the trap
that is set for me,
for you are my refuge.*
Psalm 31:3–4 NIV

Supernatural Peace

Lord, help untangle my emotions and sort my jumbled thoughts. Calm my restless spirit. Help me experience Your supernatural peace in a real and tangible way. Amen.

Gentle, Loving Hands

Heavenly Father, I long for Your peace in
my heart. Please take every anxious thread,
every tightly pulled knot of uncertainty,
sorrow, conflict, and disappointment into
Your gentle, loving hands. Amen.

Delightful Little Gifts

Father, when happiness is hard
to come by, help me to learn to
draw more consistently on Your
wellspring of joy. Help me delight
in the little gifts You bring my way
every day. Amen.

Sweet Indeed

Thank You, Lord, for teaching us that we can handle parenthood despite our fears and exhaustion.
Thank You for that first full night of sleep, which was indeed sweet. Amen.

I Will Trust

When I am afraid,
I will trust in you.
In God, whose word I praise,
in God I trust; I will not be afraid.
Psalm 56:3–4 NIV

Before I Speak

O God, help me think before I speak.
Put words of kindness in my mouth that will
build up others instead of destroying them.
I desire to be virtuous. Amen.

"Whom Shall I Fear?"

Lord, as a mother, I've often found myself afraid. Please help me remember where my strength and salvation come from and to say with confidence, "Whom shall I fear? Of whom shall I be afraid?" Amen.

All Your Cares

Lord, if I trust You for my eternal salvation, why don't I trust You for my daily needs? Instill in me the peace that comes from casting all my cares on You. Amen.

Give Joyously

Father, don't let me feel social pressure when giving. No matter how much or how little I can give, help me to give joyously. Amen.

Day 288

Teach Me Your Ways, Lord

*If you are pleased with me, teach me your
ways so I may know you and continue
to find favor with you.*

Exodus 33:13 NIV

Into My Heart

Lord, my life is full of distractions
and I have too little time to absorb
every sermon the way I should.
But You promise You will come into
my heart and live there if I welcome
You. Come into my heart,
Lord Jesus. Amen.

Words of Peace and Comfort

Lord, the next time I am angry, guide me away from sin until I can speak words of peace and comfort once again. Amen.

The Power

Lord, when my family is treated unfairly or someone judges me before knowing the whole story, I want to see justice done. Remind me to rely on You for that justice. Only You have the power to set things right once and for all. Amen.

God Can Heal Every Hurt

Father, my heart is breaking. I need to know that You are near and that You care. Gently remind me that You have the power to heal every hurt and help me make it through what I'm facing right now. Amen.

Redeem Me

*Into your hands I commit my spirit;
redeem me, O Lord, the God of truth.*
Psalm 31:5 NIV

Beyond Words

Lord, thank You for asking Jesus to
pay the high price for what I've done.
The thought of His sacrifice and Your
unending grace humbles me beyond
words. "Thank You" will never be
enough. Amen.

True Change of Heart

Father, every day is a battle. I struggle between following You and choosing what feels right at the moment. I need Your wisdom and power to persevere toward a true change of heart and action. But, most of all, I need Your forgiveness. Amen.

Angels to Watch Over Us

Heavenly Father, the world is a frightening place. I look around and see endless opportunities for disaster and tragedy. And yet, I place my trust in Your promise to send Your angels to watch over and guard me. Thank You for Your protection. Amen.

God's Protection

Lord, I know I can't hope to escape every unpleasant circumstance in this world. Just the same, I will trust in You, whatever comes. Protect me in the way You see fit, in the way that best advances Your purpose for my life. Amen.

Open My Eyes, Lord

Open my eyes that I may see wonderful things in your law.
Psalm 119:18 NIV

Take My Hand, Lord

Lord, when it comes to courage, I have none of my own. Without You, I would be filled with fear, terrified of a future I cannot see. Thank You for patiently taking my hand and helping me face my fears. Amen.

Limitless Strength

Father God, though Your strength is limitless, it's tempered with wisdom and gentleness. You are both my strong tower and my tender, loving Father. Help me to find that proper balance of gentle strength in my own life. Amen.

Cleanse Me

Father, on my worst days I feel totally unworthy. But I know You have promised to cleanse me from all unrighteousness, to wipe away my guilt and make me whole if I confess my sins. Amen.

Abundant Wisdom

Lord, life seems overwhelming to me sometimes. Please give me the abundant wisdom You've promised and help me to relax in the knowledge that You will guide me. Amen.

A Great Blessing

Father, I know it is Your will for me to understand Your Word, and You've given me the Holy Spirit to guide me. Help me to take advantage of this great blessing. Amen.

Seasoned Speech

Lord, guard my tongue as I teach my
children. Season my speech with grace—
to encourage my children and remind them
to walk in Your path. Amen.

Teach Me, Lord

Teach me, and I will be quiet;
show me where I have been wrong.
Job 6:24 NIV

Blessed Assurance

Lord, there are many forces in the world that are coming against my children and me. Your Word says that there is nothing in heaven or on earth that can separate us from Your love. Thank You for Your wonderful reassurance. Amen.

A Clear Understanding

Lord, as I read and study Your Word and hear sermons preached about it, I still have questions and much to learn. I ask that You give me a clear understanding of what You are saying to me through it. Amen.

Think, Then Speak

I'm ashamed to admit that I often speak before I think, and the words that come out of my mouth are anything but wise. Help my children to be wise enough to think first, then speak. Please help me be a good example. Amen.

Good Judgment

*Teach me knowledge
and good judgment,
for I believe in your commands.*
Psalm 119:66 NIV

An Overcomer

Lord, there are many times when I need You and Your Word to guide me. Lead me and help me become an overcomer. Amen.

The Covering of God's Blood

There is no condemnation for us when we believe in You, Jesus. The covering of Your blood helps us to prevail over anything. We never need to fear anymore. Thank You for giving us this victory.

Amen.

An Awesome God

Lord, this language I speak is so inadequate
to tell You what I want to say.
I can't begin to find the words to thank
You for the successes I have in my life.
You are awesome. Amen.

Conquerors through Christ

Lord, help me to remind my children
every day that there is nothing
ahead they need to fear.
Because of You and Your sacrifice,
we have victory. Thank You for
making us more than conquerors
through You. Amen.

Gladly Do Right

You come to the help of those
who gladly do right,
who remember your ways.
Isaiah 64:5 NIV

Complete Trust

Lord, I give all my cares to You and try to walk away, but so often I fail. I begin to fear and doubt. Forgive me, and help me to trust You completely. Amen.

Never Abandon Hope

When all hope seems lost, Lord, be with those who suffer. Help them to never abandon hope, for all things are possible with You. Amen.

Bless the Children

Father, because of Your blessings,
a tiny baby has joined us and made
us a family. May Your presence in
the midst of our family bless this
child throughout the years to come.
Amen.

Glorious Investments

Lord, You promise me wonderful rewards when I am charitable. But I cannot answer every request made of me, so I count on You to guide me as to where I should invest my efforts in such a way as to bring You glory. Amen.

The Righteous Are Blessed

Surely, O LORD, you bless the righteous;

you surround them with your favor

as with a shield.

Psalm 5:12 NIV

Weakness into Strength

Lord, show me all the good You have done
for the faithful throughout history,
and give me some of Your strength when my
own fails. Let my dependence on You turn
weakness into strength. Amen.

My Inner Strength

Lord, please increase my inner strength. Remind me that although I seem powerless, Your power knows no limits and You will provide whatever strength I need to see me through my current crisis. Amen.

Life Profit

Lord, I need Your help to learn to appreciate all that life offers, knowing there is profit in both the easy and hard times. Amen.

Eternal Care

Father, my trials are not major, so far.
But I know that things can go wrong in an
instant. When I cry to You, I know You hear.
Thank You for Your promises and never-ending
care. Amen.

Righteous Judgment

My enemies turn back;
they stumble and perish before you.
For you have upheld my right and my cause;
you have sat on your throne,
judging righteously.
Psalm 9:3-4 NIV

I Know He Loves Me

Father, I pray You will always be my rock, my salvation. Hear me when I call to You for help, for I know You love me. Amen.

Respect and Affection

Father, when I hear myself belittle my husband or speak to him harshly, remind me that Your standard for marriage is common respect and affection. I have found this man with Your help, and I love him. Amen.

Firm Yet Tender

Lord, give me wisdom and strength in my instruction to my children. Help me to be firm when I need to be, yet tender and giving as the teaching allows. Guide me in how to show love for You and Your laws. Amen.

Never-Ending Blessings

Heavenly Father, I have so much to be thankful for. My list of blessings is never ending. May I never fail to praise You and to thank You for the many blessings You have given to me. Amen.

The Wonders of God

*Many, O Lord my God,
are the wonders you have done.
The things you planned for us
no one can recount to you;
were I to speak and tell of them,
they would be too many to declare.*

Psalm 40:5 NIV

Assurance of Victory

Lord, my faith seems weak—not the type of faith that might bring victory. But in You I have the assurance of victory. I've read the story, and in the end You will reign victorious. I praise You, Lord. Amen.

Turning from Sin

Father, help me show my children the need for self-control, to not give in to the temptation of sin. Only when we turn from sin can we truly gain understanding in all wisdom. We ask for Your strength to help in this. Amen.

Like You, Jesus

True love is kind, not prideful or
self-seeking. Lord, fill me with compassion
for my fellow Christians so I might be a
godly example of love and understanding.
I want to emulate You, Jesus. Amen.

A Continuous Desire

Father, help me to be diligent
in understanding You and Your
precepts. Please give me a
continuous desire to know You
better. Amen.

Explanation of Peace

Lord, I explained peace to my children today as being a core of calm deep inside. No matter what happens to upset us on the surface, You are in our innermost being, bringing peace and comfort. Thank You that we can always trust You. Amen.

Lead Me to the Rock

From the ends of the earth I call to you,
I call as my heart grows faint;
lead me to the rock that is higher than I.

Psalm 61:2 NIV

More Like You, Lord

Lord, I know so many parents who don't
try to see things through their children's eyes
and who are not sympathetic to the trials they
face. I don't want to be like that.
Help me to be like You, Lord. Amen.

A Way of Escape

This burden is heavy, Lord.
There are days when I don't know
how much longer I can go on.
But Your Word says that You will
provide a way of escape. You help
us carry our burdens. Thank You
for Your promise. Amen.

Protection

*Father, many temptations come from
evil forces that are so deceptive they
are hard to see.
The devil fights against us daily.
Thank You for providing a way that
we can be protected from the full
assault of Satan's deceitfulness.
Amen.*

You Alone Are God

O LORD our God, deliver us from his hand,
so that all kingdoms on earth may know
that you alone, O LORD, are God.
Isaiah 37:20 NIV

Day 340

Sheep of His Pasture

Thank You, Lord, for Your love and
faithfulness to us. Thank You for making
us Your people and for allowing us to be
the sheep of Your pasture. Thank You for
allowing us to serve such a great God!
Amen.

Everlasting

Father God, the heroes my children
admire today have weaknesses.
But not You, Lord; You are perfect.
Your strength is everlasting.
Help my children to trust You as
their only hero—the One they can
trust forever and ever. Amen.

Omnipotent

*I know I can trust in You, Lord.
Thank You for Your strength that
never fails. It is there for all eternity.
You don't weaken like I do.
You are omnipotent. Amen.*

Firmly Planted

Lord, as my children grow, help me to treat them
like young trees, planting them firmly in Your
Word. Then, as I see them getting stronger every
day, I pray that they will trust You
and be blessed. Amen.

Day 344

God Is Gracious

May God be gracious to us and bless us
and make his face shine upon us,
that your ways may be known on earth,
your salvation among all nations.

Psalm 67:1-2 NIV

Keep Me Anchored

Lord, I want my heart to
continually be filled with praise
and thanksgiving to You.
Keep me anchored in the thought
that all You do is for my good and
glory. Only You are deserving of my
praise and adoration. Amen.

Delightful Prayer

Father, I thank You for answers to prayer. It is wonderful to know I have a God who delights in hearing and answering my prayers. I am glad to be able to give thanks. Amen.

Teaching God's Truths

Lord, I'm grateful that I have the opportunity to teach my children the truths that are found in Your Word. I'm trusting that You will open their spiritual understanding. I am looking forward to the day that they will accept You as Savior.

Amen.

All Glory

Lord, I pray that my children and their children and each successive generation will understand that all the glory for our many blessings belongs to You. Without You we would be nothing and would have nothing. Amen.

From Everlasting to Everlasting

*Lord, you have been our dwelling
place throughout all generations.
Before the mountains were born
or you brought forth the earth
and the world, from everlasting to
everlasting you are God.*
Psalm 90:1–2 NIV

Sufficient Strength

*Father, I praise You for Your support.
When my strength fails,
Yours is always sufficient. Thank You
for Your constant love and care,
for picking out my cry and never
failing to rescue me. Amen.*

Accepting God's Promises

Lord, help me to remember that although Your promises are free for the taking, I still need to accept them, claim them, and then live in faith that they are mine. Amen.

God's Provision

Father, I welcome Your help.
You know what I need, and I trust Your
provision, knowing You always act in
my best interests and want me to have
a happy life. Amen.

A Fruitful Vine

I want to be a fruitful vine, Lord.
With Your help I can, whether the
fruit I bring is a cheerful attitude
or money to help provide for my
family. Show me the best way to
contribute to the happiness of my
home and family. Amen.

Send Forth Your Light, Lord

Send forth your light and your truth,
let them guide me; let them bring me
to your holy mountain, to the place
where you dwell.
Psalm 43:3 NIV

Boundaries

Thank You, Father, for giving us sound doctrine.
I have boundaries set by You that I can follow
and teach to my children. All we have to do is
look to You and Your Word for guidance. Amen.

Day 356

Promise of Protection

Please protect my children, Lord.
I've tried to instill godly values,
but I can't be with them all the time.
Please send Your Spirit with them.
Keep them from being corrupted and
led away from Your truth. Amen.

New in Christ

Father, thanks to You I get to start
over, fresh and clean, because You
have made me a new person.
I now have a lifetime of new days
to spend any way I choose.
Thank You for Your never-ending
forgiveness. Amen.

Deliverance

Lord, I need deliverance from my anxiety. I am not responsible for everyone and everything—You are, and I know You are trustworthy. Help me to hope in You and trust Your protection. Amen.

Great Goodness

How great is your goodness,
which you have stored up for those who fear you,
which you bestow in the sight of men
on those who take refuge in you.

Psalm 31:19 NIV

Strengthen My Heart, Lord

Father, give me the courage I need to control my fears. I know that You love me and watch over those I love far better than I can. Strengthen my heart. Amen.

Cheerful and Kind

Lord, You welcomed me into Your family with love and acceptance. Help me be as kind to others as You have been to me—cheerfully welcoming everyone.

An Honor

Father God, it seems my cynical attitude is keeping me from performing acts of hospitality. Please give me the faith and strength to do what needs to be done, not because I want a reward but because it is an honor to do Your work. Amen.

God's Will

Father, I long to be a mother. If it is Your will, there will be children. If this is not the path You have chosen for me, I trust in You and know You will make my life meaningful in other ways.

Amen.

Day 364

A New Start

Thank You for dealing with my sins so thoroughly, Lord—for granting me a new start every day and proclaiming that I am worth saving. Amen.

Notes

Remember Me, O Lord

*Remember not the sins of my youth
and my rebellious ways;
according to your love remember me,
for you are good, O Lord.*
Psalm 25:7 NIV